A BOOK

OF

VASSAR VERSE

REPRINTS FROM
THE VASSAR MISCELLANY MONTHLY
1894-1916

PUBLISHED BY
THE VASSAR MISCELLANY MONTHLY
1916

Printing Statement:

Due to the very old age and scarcity of this book,
many of the pages may be hard to read due to the
blurring of the original text, possible missing pages,
missing text, dark backgrounds and other issues
beyond our control.

Because this is such an important and rare work, we
believe it is best to reproduce this book regardless of
its original condition.

Thank you for your understanding.

TABLE OF CONTENTS

3

AT RANDOM

PREFACE

In the selection of the verse in this volume, the editors had a twofold purpose: first and foremost to preserve verse of the highest possible standard of excellence; and secondly, to show through the collection the development of verse-making in the college since 1893, when a similar anthology was published. The poems have been arranged in chronological order, with reference to their appearance in *The Miscellany*, in order to make more evident the changing influences which have acted upon their authors, and the broadening scope of their themes. The book cannot fail to have a certain significance of symbolism, for in the lyric expression of the writers is apparent the widening range of the college girl's emotional and intellectual interest and the quickening of her contact with reality, as well as her increased power of expression.

In a measure the editors have sacrificed the historical to the aesthetic. Proportionately, recent poetry is more completely represented than that of the older magazines because it seems superior in variety and in finish. Because of this lack of proportion, the reader may not sense as keenly as did the compilers the contrast between the masses of conventional nature poetry and lullabies of the older school, and the varied richness of subject in the more modern songs. He may, however, watch imitation give way to interpretation, and thought and imagery deepen under the increasing grace of form. And he may trace to the end the spirit of courageous experiment, the reaching forth of young hands to new materials to be shaped into new forms.

The editors make no apology for including nonsense verse at the end of the volume, because it represents a definite phase of student life. To understand the life of a college without understanding the whimsies of its citizens is impossible.

The critic who condemns us for a sacrifice of dignity condemns the truthfulness of our volume. And he condemns something more—he condemns the spirit which says, "We have worked for a purpose, we have loved our work, and we have smiled."

Editors of the Vassar Miscellany Monthly 1916-1917.

A WALTZ BY CHOPIN

Far, far away
We float upon a melody of sound;
    Blue sky above us, golden light around,
And all the world one dreamy summer
    day.

Far, far away
A bird's soft note breaks o'er the water,
    clear,
    The answering song reveals his mate
    is near,
And then they join in warbling on their
    way.

Far, far away,
Soft, softer grows the tender, dual strain,
    One last, faint note responsive comes
    again,
Then silence falls. Breathless we wait
    in pain,
    But music, birds and spell have gone
    their way,
    Far, far away.

E. H. Haight, 1894.

THE MAD POET

Mad, quite mad, they tell you? Ah, poor
    fools!
They little know of what they speak.
    For see,
As no two sunsets ever were alike
Into whose gold the evening world was
    dripped,
As no two blossoms ever bloomed the
    same
Though grown so close that one the other
    touched,
So no two men. Go tell those prating
    fools
The divine difference is but more in-
    creased
Between themselves and me, and thus
    content
Their minds. * * * * * * * * * * *

If one of them had ever felt the touch
'Neath which my soul has quivered since
    its birth,

He would not call me *mad*. That yearn-
   ing love
Which is the poet's food found place in
   me;
And seized on all my little world contained
To sate itself. With Nature's smile
I smiled, and at her tears I wept. And
   then
The love I bore all things was gathered
   in
And centered on one being. Seemingly
It greater grew in its intensity,
And, looking in her eyes, I felt my heart
Swell with a passion hitherto unknown,
Swell until nigh to breaking, so that grief
Stood next to joyfulness within my love.

Once, as we played, I drew a flower across
Her smiling lips and flower-like face, and
   thought
The while, her lids were lovelier far
Than those down-drooping petals of the
   bloom;
And thereon cast the fragile thing aside,
And smiled to think how long that fairer
   flower

13

Would stay to cheer me, sent to brush
away
The blossom's gold that clung upon her
cheeks
With burning kisses. Each time when
my lips
Touched her dear face our souls seemed
made as one
And mingled in a flood of ecstasy!
Again I kissed, and held the face away
'Twixt both my hands, to view with
ravished eyes
The blushes that I knew o'erspread it.
Fiend!
What loathsome object met my madden-
ed gaze!
A face indeed—that self-same face de-
formed
By awful brands. * * * * * * * * * *

Oh Heavens! Every kiss had made a
scar!
Her eyes alone were radiant as before,
But burned into my soul. Look! See
them there—

There in that corner—here before my
     face!
Nothing but eyes, eyes, eyes—they pierce
     my flesh—
They scorch my heart out! Yes, they
     want my soul
To drag it down to Hell—O endless life
Of torture! Savage, ceaseless misery!
* * * * * * * * * * * * * *

And so men call me mad?

Nancy Vincent McClelland, 1897.

BEFORE THE DAWN

Before the dawn, when all the world's
    asleep,
And even little brooks forget to sing,
The mother moon her faithful watch must
    keep
O'er all the stars. Her task it is to bring
Her pretty children to their slumbering.
She lays aside her own bright, golden
    veil,
Then draws upon each shining baby head
A little night-cap, soft and very pale.
Soon all the sky is dark, untenanted
Before the dawn the star-babes go to bed.

M. R., 1897.

NIGHT-WIND

I called to the Night-wind, the Night-
    wind sang "No",
  Tossing the elms and the willows;
Then clasping the stars to her breast she
    swept low
  In her storm-flowing hair on the billows.

I called to the Night-wind, the Night-
    wind sighed "Yes",
  Mountain-tops golden were gleaming,
Then I gathered her hair to me, tress by
    tress,
  The stars drooped, her eyes were dream-
    ing.

Fanny Hart, 1898.

WHERE THE DEAD PAST SITS
ENTHRONED

Dark are the shadows, dark the walls of
 stone
That close about her; silence over all.
The dim light shows her regal figure, tall
And stately, seated on an ancient throne.
White-faced she is, and dead, and all
 alone.
A withered palm her nerveless hands let
 fall,
And white against the blackness of the
 wall
Shines out her hair, with cobwebs over-
 grown.
Wide are her eyes and straining through
 the gloom
Far searching always, but the rocks that
 loom
Throughout the void let never pilgrim
 nigh,
Nor voice e'er break the silence of that
 tomb,

But now and then the dead thing throned
    on high
Sends through the darkness one great,
    shuddering cry.

Emma Lou Garrett, 1899.

SUNSET

Now dark-eyed evening softly steals be-
  hind
And hides the eyes of day with her cool
  hands,
While lights and shadows play o'er mead-
  ow lands
And up the hills, at sportive hood-man-
  blind.
"Guess who am I?" with voice of mur-
  muring wind
She softly asks. He falters, "Art thou
  night?"
With loving smiles she doth his eyes un-
  bind,
Herself revealing. He, in passion bright,
Flames to an esctasy of rapturous delight.

1901.

LONELINESS

The earth's all wrapped in gray shroud-
    mist,
  Dull gray are sea and sky,
And where the water laps the land
  On gray sand-dunes stand I.
Oh, if God there be, his face from me
  The rolling gray mists hide;
And if God there be, his voice from me
  Is kept by the moan of the tide.

Adelaide Crapsey, 1901.

WITH THE PASSING OF THE SUN

Dead is the sun king on his royal couch
Of gold and purple; and the night monks
    come
And silently creep near it, one by one,
And, sombre-robed, uplift their taper
    stars.
And in the darkness chant a requiem.

Emma Lou Garrett, 1899.

A FRAGMENT

(Supposed continuation of line 277, Book V, Odyssey)

And Calypso, fair among nymphs, lovely
    with grace of goddess,
Stood on the sands of the sea-beach and
    gazed far out on the ocean.
There on the dark-colored sea, like a bird
    on the high-vaulted heaven,
Sped the great barge of Odysseus, tossed
    by the surge of the waters.
Smaller and smaller it grew, till at last
    she could see it no longer.
There sat she down and wept, mournful
    she was, and despairing;
Slowly the stars came out like torches
    proclaiming the night-fall,
Shining till dimmed by Aurora, they sank
    to their bath in the billows.

But Calypso, fair among nymphs, sat
on the sands of the sea-beach,
Weeping and hiding her face from the sight
of the pitiless ocean.

Evelina Pierce, 1902.

DUTCH TULIPS

Acres of glowing color
Stretching from dyke to stream,
Lifting their blazing torches
Bright as a fleeting dream;
Like a flush of rose on the meadows,
Or a blot of blood-red wine,
Or a flaming field of cloth-of-gold,
Is Holland, in tulip time!

Mary Atwater Mason, 1902.

NOVEMBER

Quiet, at peace, in silent strength she
    stands,
The dull wind blowing on her rugged
    face,
Roughing her heavy hair; with sombre
    grace
Tall, leafless branches sway in her strong
    hands;
The rude burrs catch her dress, and thorny
    vines
Touched with the last deep color of the
    year
Cling to its hem, faded and frayed and
    sear,
Fringing the coarse, dusk folds with
    fragile spines.
A look far-seeing fills her wide, deep eyes,
And the still light of long, gray after-
    noon.

Bravely she waits the future, asks no
    boon,
Hers the year's precious past, its golden
    memories.

Letitia Jean Smyth, 1901.

SPRING SONG

The glad, mad hills
All veined with rills,
Are glowing a glory
Of infinite green,
And a lyric laughter flashes round
With the onyx-emerald sheen.

To the birch foam toss,
To the throb of the glade,
To the pulse of the wheat,
To the surge of the blade,
To the beat of the flood,
To the reel of the blood,
Dance! lilt! swing!
And off! Awing
With the gold-throat oriole.

Mary Fleming, 1902.

THROUGH WINTER WOODS

Gray mottled beech trunks locked in snow,
And a muffled stillness all around;
A stillness cut with the little smack
Of a tiny twig a-springing back
As a ball of snow with a breathy sound
Drops from the iced green pines bent low.

Pale yellow shafts on a snow blue-white
And a molten sun behind the hill;
And thickening shadows under the trees
And the sharp little sting of a sudden
     breeze,
As up from the crackled crusted rill
Comes the clean-cut breath of the winter's
     night.

Margaret Adelaide Pollard, 1902.

THE SEER

To dwell alone in countries of the sun;
To go all uncompanioned in the light;
To see the valleys from a windy height,
And long to rest therein, day being done.
To weary of the beauties, one by one,
That shine across the air too bleakly
    bright;
To be too close upon the stars by night.
And, lonely as the peak, abide thereon!

Immortal mind and mortal heart that
    yearns,
Grave wondrous soul to whom God speaks
    his word,
The skies are cold, and earth is warm with
    love!
Come for a space to where the hearth-
    fire burns.
And then if God's own voice should sound
    unheard!
Nay, thou shalt watch and wait and
    dream thereof.

Mary Burt Messer, S.

WHITE WINGS

She lingered for a while beside life's sea,
Gathering strange, lovely thoughts to
    string like shells
In lyric lengths of song,
Numbering the rhythmic beating of the
    deep,
Watching the soft, clear day steal from
    the east,
Or westward fading, touch the crinkling
    waves
With tender glory; and she saw the boats
Glide with ribbed sails across the sun,
    and flit
Whit'ning through the blue distance,
    where afar
The heavenly country lies all wrapped
    in mist.
There most of all she gazed, and if a
    gleam
Threaded the mist, her passionate, grave
    eyes

With more than earthly lustre caught its
    light;
Thus did she live until her soul took wing
And vanished, like some white bird, in
    the blue.

Elsie Mitchell Rushmore, 1906.

SONG OF AN IRISH MOTHER

Out 'cross the swamp and the mire
The weirdies are flashin' their fire,
An' down in the log-wood the soft rains
    are fallin',
Where the wee lonesome fairies are callin'
    and callin',
    With voices that sound like yours,
    With voices that sound like yours.

Your daddy's old pipe's gettin' low,
Where he sits in the hearth-fire's glow,
And all 'round the thatch-roof the rain
    spirit's swishin'
While I'm waitin' here, darlin', a wishin'
    an' wishin'
    You were back in this cradle o' yours,
    You were back in this cradle o' yours.

Olive Stewart, 1908.

ELEMENTAL

There are five elements of which all existing things are composed,—Earth, Air Fire, Water, and Ether

Japanese Legend.

Driven wind on the gray hill's crest,
Wandering breeze in the green marsh
grass;

Measureless height and endless reach,
Deepening blue of the open sky;

Flame,—the sweep of a red-hot scourge,
And the licking tongue of the leaping fire:

Frolic of water over the stones;
Limpid depths of a quiet pool:

The odor of fresh-turned earth in spring,
Warm and virile and rich with life.

Passionate, vivid, wayward, free,
Beloved, you're all of the world to me.

Eliza Adelaide Draper, 1907.

34

THE CHORUS

Whisper to the moon-gleam,
  Whisper to the sea,
Whisper to the moonbeam,
  Follow, follow me.

When the wind is in the willows,
  And the fireflies in the glen,
And the moonlight on the pillows
  Of sleep-enamoured men,—

When the elves are in the forest,
  Seeking starshine in the dew,
And their tiny tunes are chorused
  Where the starlight filters through;

Then, whisper to the moon-gleams,
  Whisper to the sea,
Whisper to the moonbeams,
  Follow, follow me.

Louise Medbery, 1907.

A PAGAN

I am a pagan, I!
I worship earth and sun and sea and sky;
I hold no faith, expressed in mankind's
    words.
My creed comes to me in the song of
    birds,
And waving grasses, and the sun's glad
    light,
And strong, high hills and rivers, silver-
    bright,
And soft, still clouds that silently float
    by, —
I am a pagan, I!

I never wonder why
All men are born to sin, and then to die.
I only love the whole great world around,
And revel in its joy of sight and sound.
I love it all,—I love, and long to praise
The strange, great unknown Soul of it
    always,

The Soul of earth and sun and sea and
   sky,—
Am I a pagan, I?

Beatrice Daw, 1909.

ON THE COAST OF MAINE

I.

Off-Shore

The dappled blue of the evening sky,
  With the cloud-rack in the west,
All purpled bright in the living light,
  Like the Islands of the Blest.

And out of the islands sweeps the wind
  As much as the sails can hold,
As we race home through the rustling foam
  And the grey waves laced with gold.

II.

In the Fog

The cool grey wraps us more and more,
  Our slack sail lifts to the fitful wind,
  And I see through the rift where the
    fog has thinned
The floating ghost of the distant shore.

III.

On the Sand-Bar

The curdling foam on the blue-black
    sands,
    The lap and splash of the rising tide,
    As it slowly creeps to the farther side,
Where the lone tree stretches its ghostly
    hands.

IV.

A Summer Storm

A leaden sea and a silver sky,
    A line of light at the sunset edge,
Long wisps of cloud go drifting by,
    While the white foam licks at the rocky
        ledge.

Then the shouting sea-wind takes its toll?
    From the moaning forest's pain,
And the storm sweeps by with the thun-
    der's roll,
    And the rattle of the rain.

V.

In the Pine-Woods

The sunlight through the pines
    Touches the mossy stones with living
    green,
And marks the silver lines
    Left where the fairy spinner's way has
    been.

With tender murmuring
    The fragrant breezes steal from tree to
    tree,
And now the vagrants bring
    The vital freshness of the distant sea.

VI.

Outward-Bound

The schooner's sail is slack and drawn
    And the schooner's wheel is still,
And the sick prow lifts through the shift-
    ing seas,
    Like a thing bereft of will.

For the grey fog wraps us round, my lads,
  And the good ship needs must stay,
Then hey and ho! for the bonny breeze,
  That drives the fog away.

There's a crinkling over the sluggish
    waves,
  A whispering in the sail,
And the schooner turns like a tired dog,
  At the sound of his master's hail.

For the grey fog lifts off-shore, my lads,
  And the good ship bounds away.
Then hey and ho! for the bonny breeze
  That drives the fog away.

Louisa Brooke, 1907.

TO-NIGHT LIFE'S WEB SEEMED TWISTED ALL AWRY

To-night life's web seemed twisted all
  awry,
Its faded colors trampled in the ground,
Till here, within the darkening woods, I
  found
This quiet pool beneath the starlit sky.
The waters deeply still, the lissome reeds
Scarce ruffling its smooth surface, the low,
  soft
Monotonous murmur of the pines aloft,
The very air a sweet contentment breeds.
Above, a heron floats on softened wing.
Deep in the woods a liquid-thrilling
  thrush
Voices the dumb souled Night. And
  through the hush
I feel your great, calm spirit comforting.
The tangled webs grow straight. And
  now we seem
Together, 'neath the stars, to sit and
  dream.   *Dorothea Gay, 1911.*

WHERE THE WAVES MEET THE SHORE

My fingers touch the cool, firm sand,
They let it sift between them, lovingly.
The little waves, with rhythmic melody,
Hush, and whisper, and break forth in
    gentle song,
As they plash in and out;
As each recedes, the uncovered beach
Is quickened with a life from out the west,
And—like the dew drops on the faery
    webs
That breathe with color in the early morn—
Each moment it receives the warm caress
Of that far, radiant space beyond the sea,
And, shimmering momently, gives back
A quiet answer, with a flush
Of soft dream fire.

Katherine Taylor, 1910.

CHRISTMAS

Mother, just listen—town is sparkly
   bright,
   And windows full of gorgeous things,
And holly, bundles, people—Oh, I saw
   Such cunning angel's wings.

But out doors here it is so very still,
   My stars are smiling far away,
I can't tell why,—and then the little wind
   Just kissed me, and won't say.

Mother, you're smiling like the people
   too,
   And like the little wind, and why
Am I so very happy—just so glad,
   And inside want to cry?

Sarah Hincks, 1910.

FLUCTUATION

It lies o'er grain-fields surging in the
    breeze;
  On the dim wood-path in the glancing
    shift
Of sunlight falling through the air-stirred
    trees;
  Or on the ocean in the breathless lift
Of moon-tracked swells not risen to a
    wave;
  In autumn leaves revolving as they
    drift;
In eyes, as Dante calls them, "slow and
    grave";
  In smiles of earnest men and human
    seers.—
A certain rhythmic play of light and shade
  That weaves the shimmering fabric
    of our years.

Hazel Bishop Poole, 1909.

THE SEA-SHORE

The sun is warm upon my back,
As warm as mother's hand,
And where I've dug my well to-day
'There's water in the sand.

The Chinese boys down underneath,
Are they as warm as me?
The water half-way down my well
Is cold as it can be.

Ruth Elizabeth Presley, 1909.

IN THE HOSPITAL

These days when I am sick in bed—
I've been in bed so long you know—
I lie and listen to the steps
And wonder where they go.

They hurry past out on the walk
And hurry up the empty street,
They're going home's *fast* they can,
I know those happy feet.

Sometimes out in the corridor
A nurse goes by with slow, soft slide;
Sometimes she hurries—then I know
Some boy like me, has died.

Ruth Elizabeth Presley, 1909.

SUMMER WINDS

They rush along, the daughters of the
  wind,
Grey-eyed, strong-limbed, their dust-
  brown hair swirled back.
The children of the great warm west are
  they.
One, high among the white cloud domes
  that hang
So lazy in the sky, stirs them to life.
Another skims across the grass that bends
In silver waves beneath her scarce-felt
  tread.
Then, darting up, past twinkling maple
  leaves,
Bows down the tall elm's crown.
But onward, ever onward still they rush,
And meeting in the wood, sigh through
  the pines
And pass and leave behind in drowsy
  heat,
A breathless calm, close-wrapping like a
  shroud.   *Margaret Adams Hobbs*, 1910.

48

FLITTER-MOTH

On the road to—Anywhere!—once I met
   her singing;
  Such a little elf was she,
  Winsome, full of witchery,
  Shy as any sprite could be,—
Dancing, flitting, winging.

On the road to—Anywhere!—over hill
   and hollow,
  Where the little witch demure,
  Ever beckoning, doth lure,
  Weary, humble and obscure,
I, her pilgrim, follow.

On the road to—Anywhere!—I will ne'er
   forsake her.
  Though the little witch may be
  Naught but errant Fantasy,
  Though she flout and mock at me,
I will overtake her.

Genevieve J. Williams, 1911.

MORNING ON THE RIVER

The river moves in silvery expanse,
Soft-brushed with early mist along its
    shores,
Whose peaceful slopes lie slumbering dim
    and gray,—
While far above one glistening white gull
    soars.

Helen Lathrop, 1911.

THE POET'S MISTRESS SINGS

My love is not as other lovers are—
He comes to me from planets more re-
    mote;
The voice of distant worlds is in his
    throat,
His eyes have caught the light of some
    strange star.

Such gifts he brings as queens in vain de-
    sire,
Proud queens, for all their crowns of
    carven gold,
Their silken robes, in lustrous fold on fold,
For all their gems that flame like frozen
    fire.   ▲

Their hearts cry vainly for the gifts he
    brings—
Wild, winged songs that soar and flash
    and fall,

Dark, splendid songs, and beautiful and
small
Sweet songs that softly to my heart he
sings.

For through the circling worlds he takes
his flight,
Seeking rare songs, that I, his love, may
be
Clothed in the subtle splendor of the sea,
Crowned with the ancient glory of the
night.

Genevieve J. Williams, 1911.

EXILE

Alfalfa fields, at twilight purple-gray,
Where western prairie bounds the curve
    of sky,—
A narrow road that has nor tree nor bend,
A toiler from the mill who passes by.

A figure with a tinge of Old World grace,
Deep color in the kerchief knotted free,
Young eyes that hold a hint of Athens'
    gleam,—
A longing for a sunlit, azure sea.

Marion Eleanor Crampton, 1911.

THE KNOT-HOLE

There's a whiff of dust comin' down the
    road,
    It's fairies in dust clouds that's
    blowin',
Find a knot-hole to look at them through,
    boyneen,
    And their errand you'll be knowin'.

'Tis I had better be lookin' myself,
    Wurra, be keepin' behind—
When the Little Men catch your eye
    through the knot,
    'Tis the black curse they give, strike
    you blind.

If they should bring me a changeling,
    now,
    'Tis a trouble for some one they're
    bearin',
See the crooked, dancin' legs on them,
    And the scraps of coats they're wearin'.

Mother Mercy, did one of them see me
    then?
The crowd's gettin' distant and far,
The corn crake is cryin'—it's day then,
    sure,
Boyneen, where is it you are!

Margaret Frances Culkin, 1912.

SAXON LULLABY

Folded asleep are the hawthorne blows,
And faint on the evening wind is the rose.
Wriggle no more, little son, be still,
For the Lord of Dreams waits here at the
    sill.
    By-low-low.

Thou shalt ride this night on a milk-
    white steed,
Shod by Weland with shoes of speed,
Adown the gleaming Roman road,
Its border with scarlet dream-blooms
    sowed,
And the wind shall whistle through thy
    locks—
But when thou hearest the surf on the
    rocks.
Draw rein and remember thy mother at
    home.

Draw rein, turn back oh son of mine!
Though sky is blue and white sails shine,

Though the ring-necked ships do thee
    courtesy,
And in homage the sea-birds dip to the
    sea.
Trust not the slow waves heaving black;
More men go out than e'er come back
Over the gannet—road to Rome.

So, so! I meant not to fright thee, hush!
The linnet is singing good-night to the
    thrush.
All out of doors is drowsy and gray,
And I wait to speed thee on thy way.
    By-low-low.

Dorothea Gay, 1911.

AFTERWARDS

I think you sent the withered leaves
   That blew all day across the grass,
All day, all day they rustled by,
   A tattered, flying mass.

For all the world was whirling leaves
   Against the lonely, wind-swept sky,
And every leaf was whispering
   Your name as it flew by.

Tonight the leaves lie quietly,
   Sodden and still beneath the rain
That drums along the eaves, and drives
   Against the window pane.

Genevieve J. Williams, 1911.

QUEEN'S LACE

Child! how high the brown weeds stand,
Reaching up to touch your hand!
Round your knees the Queen's lacedry
Holds up cups as you pass by.
You, who see the tiny elves
In those seed-cups rock themselves,
Tell the flowers to love me too,
Reaching cups to me as you!

Frances Shriver, 1911.

FROM THE DUSK

The dark'ning road had hidden you; I
  turned
In dread to see the home we loved, but
  watched
The garden changed to spirit; tinged trees
That rose across the mist, or glowed like
  cloud
About the lamps; a vague dim sky that
  made
All distance nothing, even absence all
Mistaken fear; then felt you close and
  groped—
And struck my hand against the iron
  gate.

Elizabeth Toof, 1913.

PIERRETTE

Ah, Pierrette! I see thee dance
Amid the maskers gay.
With piquant poise, with witching glance,
As sweetly pale a face
As an arbutus bud in May,
Save for the scarlet lips,
So laughing light with wind-swayed grace
Through music's maze you trip.

Ah, Pierrette! I know thy heart,
A burning crimson rose
By folly's rude hand plucked apart
To many a bleeding shred,
Robbed of its bloom by sorrow's snows.
One night when I was near,
"Ah, God! I wish that I were dead,"
You whispered in my ear.

Helen Clark, 1913.

THE WIND SONG

I am the child of the sea—
I sweep the purple fog on its landward
    track,
I cry in the thundering roar of the ocean
    surge,
I beat the crests of the towering waves to
    foam,
And dash them down to burst on the angry
    reefs;
I tear the sea-weed black from the salt-
    sprayed rock,
I lash the stark brown cliffs with hissing
    surf,
I toss and buffet the treasure-laden
    ships,
And strip the taut-stretched sail from the
    shivering mast,
And strew the waste of waves with their
    golden spoils,
And hurl them up to rot on the strangers'
    shore,
And mock at the hopes of men.

I am the child of the land—
I whistle in whirling dust through the
    city street,
I shriek through the rigid frame of slen-
    der steel,
Looming black and bare to the cold green
    sky;
I batter the thousand panes with shower
    of hail,
Sweeping the roof and the cornice heaped
    with snow;
I blow o'er the rolling prairies' inland sea,
Where the fields of corn lie red in the
    evening light,
And the deepening purple shadows creep
    to the east,
As the curling smoke cloud beckons the
    laborer home;
I rush o'er the western ranges wide and
    clear,
With the sage brush green and gray in the
    morning sun,
The rock-red soil and the brown of the
    stunted pine;
I sing in the rhythmic beat of the broncho's
    hoofs,

The blast of the surging stream that
seeks for gold,
The thud of the axe as it swings in the
clearing green;
I moan through the desert's awful silences,
Where the cold gray rocks, 'mid the miles
of barren brush,
From a level sea loom gaunt to the ghostly
moon;
I howl in the roar of the train with its
shower of fire,
The piercing engine's shriek through the
black ravine,
The wild coyote's cry to the lonely stars;
I sweep o'er the empty wastes of sand,
and yearn
For the finite souls of men.

Henriette de Saussure Blanding, 1912.

AFTER THE SEASON

Untrampled lies the sand, smooth, hard
   and clean,
   Scattered with gleaming yellow cockle
   shells
   And bits of grey drift-wood. The cool
   air smells
Freshly of salt, most when the wind blows
   keen
From off south-lying fishing banks. Se-
   rene
   The pale blue sky bends down to meet
   the swells
   That set the buoys aswing and toll the
   bells,
Then break upon the bar, wild white and
   green.
The bathing beach is marked by rope-
   less posts;
   The vacant board-walk stretches dull
   and bare.
   The Old Casino's shuttered windows
   stare

Half-crazed by sighing of the uneasy
    ghosts
Of tunes the band used, summer long,
    to play,—
Far out at sea one ship's smoke fades
    away.

Helen Dorothea Romer, 1912.

SLEEP SONG OF THE PINES

Dimness and dusky bars
Drift on the branches' light;
Dearer than song are stars,
Dearer than day is night.

Moon-quivers pale and long
Meet on the mosses gray.
Dearer is dream than song,
Dearer is night than day.

Elizabeth Toof, 1913.

TRISTRAM

For me, Iseult, the shadows of your hair
Hold all the dusky sweetness of the night,
Your eyes the joy of all the shining stars.
Deep in your voice the comfort of the rain,
The warmth and vibrant stillness of noon
    suns
Lie folded, as in promise of the Spring.
I can not let you go! Your loss would be
The loss of all the meaning that is Life.

Yet—sometimes when the night wind holds her breath
    holds her breath
A voice cries through the darkness: "*This*
    is Death!"

Elizabeth Mason Heath, 1916.

68

ALYTH

Naked as sun-fleck she treads the brook,
   Trailing the water weed tangled there;
Glows of her hair make the shadows blind;
   Teased by her laughter the winds des-
      pair.

Stain of the rushes and tear of thorn
   Darken her feet in the water's flow;
Glimmers that fall from her breast and
      hair
   Mingle and stir like a lily's glow.

Elizabeth Toof, 1913.

WINDS AND THE LILIES

I wish I were the wind that blows
In the wood-lilies,
And bends and breaks them and then
    goes.
What of the broken lilies then? Who
    knows,
For who thinks twice of anything the
    wind
Has torn and thinned!
Deep golden petals scattered on the air
Drift here and there—
Deep tawny golden—more like Inyr's
    hair
Than anything I've dreamed of; she is
    pale
And slim and frail
As the slenderest lily-stalks Heaven knows.

I wish I were the wind that blows
In the wood-lilies
And bends and breaks them and then
    goes.

Helen Lombaert Scobey, 1913.

FROM HOMER

"Homer, thy song men liken to the sea,
With every note of music in his tone,
With tides that wash the wide dominion
Of Hades, and light waves that lash in
    glee,
Around the isles enchanted. * * * * *"

Before me sweeps the dark and widening
    sea
And wistfully, I strain my eyes across the
    waves
To glimpse the sturdy, wing-sailed ship
    that bears
My son again to Ithaca * * * a fair
    haired lad,
Boy to the battle-famed Odysseus, who
    had
But lately left his play, to sail
To far off Ilium, o'er the deep'ning sea.
How long the years have been; how
    heavy-winged!

71

The lad mayhap has changed; his eyes
    less young,
His voice less full of joyous mirth;
His heart—oh Zeus immortal, give to me
His heart as sweet, as when he played at
    ball
Beside me in the sunny megaron * * * *
While I plied back and forth to spin for
    him
A kiton from new-carded wool * * * * *
How long the watch is; and how dark the
    sea.

Rebecca Park Lawrence, 1913.

A PRAYER TO BUDDHA

The wind has blown against my face
A leaf of mist-wet bloom.

In calm of depthless thinking, look forever
Upon the leaves of lake-lapped lotus
flowers,
No chanting from thy temples break thy
musing;
Nor prayer bells mark the silence into hours.

But when the smoke of sandal-wood is
rising
From Temples where the throbs of chant-
ing cease,—
Because that scent once stilled thy prayer
to silence,
Upon thy people lay the spell of peace.

The wind has blown against my face
A leaf of mist-wet bloom.

Elizabeth Toof, 1913.

THE ABBEY BELLS OF MIDDEL-
BURG

At Middelburg the night drags slow
Because the chimes are never still,
But mark the quarters as they go
With carillons unending, shrill.
You hear the bells at Middelburg,
The Abbey bells of Middelburg,
Until it seems the live-long night
Is full of bells at Middelburg.

You may have visions between bells
Of Rosendaal with hedge-rimmed fields,
Or Dort with Docks, or somewhere else
With long low-lying poppy fields,
Or Domburg's dykes and windmill wings—
But these are visions that give place
As night creeps on to sadder things,
While quarters drag and bells keep pace.

When hope is dead and sleep is vain.
And thoughts are mad, but dreams are
    worse,

And every chime smites like a pain,
And carillons become a curse,
You hear the bells at Middelburg,
The shrill high bells at Middelburg,
Until you think the live-long night
Is cursed with bells at Middelburg.

Helen Lombaert Scobey, 1913.

TO A STRANGER

I have seen you arise and go forth in the
    night
And run up a white winding way
To the top of a hill, through the grass un-
    der stars,
Where you chased the wild wind in your
    play.

You were mad when you tossed back your
    bare head and laughed,
When you caught at a star in its fall,
It changed to a glimmering moth and
    flew by,—
O tonight, when you pass, will you call?

Ruth Thomas Pickering, 1914.

LOVE SONG

I love you with a heart that dances in
the sunshine,
That sings the strangest wildness of a
wild blue wave,
That trembles in the fierce sweep of a
green streaked wind storm,
When pine trees break and lost birds cry,
and sky-topped rock cliffs cave.

I wait for you where clouds stretch pale
and far off northward.
Where fruits red ripe are hanging breath-
less in noon light,
Where yellow birds are flying over purple
flowers.
Where grasses blow with restless yearn-
ing all the long white night.

Ruth Thomas Pickering, 1914.

O, I WENT DOWN TO THE RIVER BANK

O, I went down to the river bank
Last night
When a million stars were bright
And you in the long grass lay.

O, the wind blew over the river bank
Last night
And the touch of your lips was light
As we in the long grass lay.

O, I came up from the river bank
Alone,
While the weary wind made moan
And the dawn on the crushed grass lay.

Ruth Thomas Pickering, 1914.

EVENING

When Evening first, rising from day-long
    rest,
Cups her slow hands 'round Day's too
    dazzling light,
Still through her fingers slips a radiance
    bright
Reddening and spreading in the darken-
    ing west.
She sighs; and in the fragrant dusk, the
    breeze
Makes whispered music through the qui-
    vering trees;
Then strengthening Night snuffs out the
    Day's last spark
And sets the first star shimmering in the
    dark.

Carolyn Crosby Wilson, 1917.

PERSEPHONE TO ORPHEUS

I do remember now a far off day
And long-forgotten in this frozen place,—
A gleam of sunlit flowers, wet with spray,
And the long sea beach whitening for
    a space
Between the green land and the purple
    sea.
The black car hurtles through the startled
    air.
Forever mingled with my young despair
The sharp tang of the sea-salt strangles
    me.
Singer, your song has waked to life again
The dear lost gift of tears, and all the
    whirl
Of quick-pulsed love and hatred.   Sweet
    is pain
To one long dead to passion,—Take the
    girl!

Elizabeth Mason Heath, 1916.

80

INTERIM

A man speaks

The room is full of you!—As I came in
And closed the door behind me, all at once
A something in the air, intangible,
Yet stiff with meaning, struck my senses
    sick!—
Sharp, unfamiliar odors have destroyed
Each other room's dear personality.
The heavy scent of damp, funereal flowers,
The very essence, hush-distilled, of Death,
Has strangled that habitual breath of
    home
Whose expiration leaves all houses dead;
And whereso'er I look is hideous change.
Save here. Here 'twas as if a weed-
    choked gate
Had opened at my touch, and I had step-
    ped
Into some long-forgot, enchanted, strange,
Sweet garden of a thousand years ago

And suddenly thought, "I have been here
    before!"

You are not here.   I know that you are
    gone,
And will not ever enter here again.
And yet it seems to me, if I should speak,
Your silent step must wake across the
    hall;
If I should turn my head, that your sweet
    eyes
Would kiss me from the door.—So short
    a time
To teach my life its transposition to
This difficult and unaccustomed key!—

The room is as you left it; your last touch
A thoughtless pressure, knowing not it-
    self
As saintly—hallows now each simple
    thing;
Hallows and glorifies, and glows between
The dust's gray fingers like a shielded
    light.

There is your book, just as you laid it
    down,

82

Face to the table,—I cannot believe
That you are gone!—Just then it seemed
    to me
You must be here. I almost laughed to
    think
How like reality the dream had been;
Yet knew before I laughed, and so was
    still.

That book, out-spread, just as you laid
    it down!
Perhaps you thought, "I wonder what
    comes next,
And whether this or this will be the end,"
So rose and left it, thinking to return.

Perhaps that chair, when you arose and
    passed
Out of the room, rocked silently a while
Ere it again was still. When you were
    gone
Forever from the room, perhaps that
    chair,
Stirred by your movement, rocked a little
    while,
Silently to and fro * * * * * * * * * *

And here are the last words your fingers
    wrote,
Scrawled in broad characters across a
    page
In this brown book I gave you. Here
    your hand,
Guiding your rapid pen, moved up and
    down.
Here with a looping knot you crossed a
    "t",
And here another like it, just beyond
These two eccentric "e's". You were
    so small,
And wrote so brave a hand!
                        How strange it seems
That of all words these are the words
    you chose!
And yet a simple choice; you did not
    know
You would not write again. If you had
    known—
But then, it does not matter,—and in-
    deed,
If you had known there was so little time
You would have dropped your pen and
    come to me,

And this page would be empty, and some
   phrase
Other than this would hold my wonder
   now.
Yet, since you could not know, and it
   befell
That these are the last words your fingers
   wrote,
There is a dignity some might not see
In this, "I picked the first sweet-pea to-
   day."

To-day! Was there an opening bud be-
   side it
You left until tomorrow?—O, my love,
The things that withered,—and you came
   not back!
That day you filled the circle of my arms
That now is empty. (O, my empty life!)
That day—that day you picked the first
   sweet-pea,—
And brought it in to show me! I recall
With terrible distinctness how the smell
Of your cool gardens drifted in with you.
I know, you held it up for me to see

And flushed because I looked not at the
flower
But at your face; and when behind my
look
You saw such unmistakable intent.
You laughed and brushed your flower
against my lips.
(You were the fairest thing God ever
made,
I think.) And then your hands above
my heart
Drew down its stem into a fastening,
And while your head was bent I kissed
your hair.

I wonder if you knew. (Beloved hands!
Somehow I cannot seem to see them
still.
Somehow I cannot seem to see the dust
In your bright hair.) What is the need
of Heaven
When earth can be so sweet?—If only
God
Had let us love,—and show the world the
way!

Strange cancelings must ink the eternal
    books
When love-crossed-out will bring the
    answer right!

That first sweet pea! I wonder where it
    is.
It seems to me I laid it down somewhere,
And yet,—I am not sure. I am not sure,
Even, if it was white or pink; for then
'Twas much like any other flower to me,
Save that it was the first. I did not
    know,
Then, that it was the last. If I had
    known—
But then it does not matter. Strange
    how few,
After all's said and done, the things that
    are
Of moment.
    Few indeed! When I can make
Of ten small words a rope to hang the
    world!
"I had you and I have you now no more."

There, there it dangles,—where's the
    little truth
That can for long keep footing under
    that
When its slack syllables tighten to a
    thought?
Here, let me write it down! I wish to
    see
Just how a thing like that will look on
    paper!

"I had you and I have you now no more."

O, little words, how can you run so
    straight
Across the page, beneath the weight you
    bear?
How can you fall apart, whom such a
    theme
Has bound together, and hereafter aid
In trivial expression that have been
So hideously dignified?—Would God
That tearing you apart would tear the
    thread

I strung you on! Would God—O, God,
    my mind
Stretches asunder on this merciless rack
Of imagery! O, let me sleep awhile!
Would I could sleep, and wake to find me
    back
In that sweet summer afternoon with
    you.
Summer? 'Tis summer still by the calen-
    dar!
How easily could God, if he so willed,
Set back the world a little turn or two!
Correct its griefs, and bring its joys
    again!

We were so wholly one I had not thought
That we could die apart. I had not
    thought
That I could move,—and you be stiff and
    still!
That I could speak,—and you perforce
    be dumb!
I think our heart-strings were, like warp
    and woof
In some firm fabric, woven in and out;

Your golden filaments in fair design
Across my duller fibre. And today
The shining strip is rent; the exquisite
Fine pattern is destroyed; part of your
    heart
Aches in my breast; part of my heart lies
    chilled
In the damp earth with you. I have been
    torn
In two, and suffer for the rest of me.

What is my life to me? And what am I
To life,—a ship whose star has guttered
    out?
A Fear that in the deep night starts awake
Perpetually, to find its senses strained
Against the taut strings of the quivering
    air,
Awaiting the return of some dread chord?

Dark, Dark, is all I find for metaphor;
All else were contrast,—save that con-
    trast's wall
Is down, and all opposed things flow to-
    gether

Into a vast monotony; where night
And day, and frost and thaw, and death
    and life,
Are synonyms. What now—what now
    to me
Are all the jabbering birds and foolish
    flowers
That clutter up the world? You were
    my song!
Now, now let discord scream! You were
    my flower!
Now let the world grow weeds! For I
    shall not
Plant things above your grave; (the com-
    mon balm
Of the conventional woe for its own
    wound!)
Amid sensations rendered negative
By your elimination stands to-day,
Certain, unmixed, the element of grief;
I sorrow; and I shall not mock my truth
With travesties of suffering, nor seek
To effigy its incorporeal bulk
In little wry-faced images of woe.

I cannot call you back; and I desire

No utterance of my material voice.
I cannot even turn my face this way
Or that, and say, "My face is turned to
    you;"
I know not where you are, I do not know
If Heaven hold you or if earth transmute,
Body and soul, you into earth again;
But this I know:—not for one second's
    space
Shall I insult my sight with visionings
Such as the credulous crowd so eager-
    eyed
Beholds, self-conjured, in the empty air.
Let the world wail! Let drip its easy
    tears!
My sorrow shall be dumb!
What do I say?
God! God!—God pity me! Am I gone mad
That I should spit upon a rosary?
Am I become so shrunken? Would to
    God
I too might feel that frenzied faith whose
    touch
Makes temporal the most enduring grief;
Tho' it must walk a while, as is its wont,

With wild lamenting! Would I too might
  weep
Where weeps the world and hangs its
  piteous wreaths
For its new dead! Not Truth, but Faith,
  it is
That keeps the world alive. If all at
  once
Faith were to slacken,—that unconscious
  faith
Which must, I know, yet be the corner-
  stone
Of all believing—, birds now flying fearless
Across would drop in terror to the earth;
Fishes would drown; and the all-govern-
  ing reins
Would tangle in the frantic hands of God
And the worlds gallop headlong to des-
  truction!

O, God I see it now,, and my sick brain
Staggers and swoons! How often over me
Flashes this breathlessness of sudden
  sight
In which I see the universe unrolled

Before me like a scroll and read thereon
Chaos and Doom, where helpless planets
    whirl
Dizzily round and round and round and
    round,
Like tops across a table, gathering speed
With every spin, to waver on the edge
One instant—looking over—and the next
To shudder and lurch forward out of
    sight—
            * * * * * * * *
Ah, I am worn out—I am wearied out—
It is too much—I am but flesh and blood,
And I must sleep.   Tho' you were dead
    again,
I am but flesh and blood and I must sleep.

Edna St. Vincent Millay, 1917.

SWING IN THE SWING

Swing in the swing and imagine,
Swing in the swing and suppose,
'Magine if I was a lady
Havin' a train to my clothes,

I'd never stop eating candy,
I'd never go up to bed,
And when they talked about secrets
I wouldn't be sent on ahead.

Swing in the swing and imagine,
Swing in the swing and p'tend,
Swing in the swing and whoop-ti-oh—
Jump to the ground in the end.

Vivian Gurney, 1915.

THE APPRENTICE

The devil take these foolish meek mad-
    onnas—
Their simpering smiles! Pray look at
    this one now
There, grinning in the darkness, on her
    brow
The crown of heaven, and that silly face
Such as the people like to see, the fools!
Gemma who sells the flowers on the bridge
And those girls washing linen in the pools
Have more of life, of beauty, of true grace,
Well fit to be God's mother. Andrea
Knows how to please the populace. I
    hear
Him bargaining "Mother and Child, so
    much
And so much added for each saint "—he's
    dear—
It's just like selling cloth. Passion of
    God!
To sell your soul by the square foot! and
    yet

It would not be so hard could I forget
That damned soft smile on angel, saint
    and queen;
If I could bring in Gemma for an hour
And sing to her the song I learned last
    night,
And while she laughed out loud, had I
    the power,
I'd paint her in, large-mouthed, and
    strong and keen
If not as Mary, at least, Magdalene.

Elizabeth Jane Coatsworth, 1915.

CHANSON

My melody at first was slow and round:
Then, breaking too much sweetness, a
  great chord
Crashed out, swept up, and all its color
  poured
Into a slender, dwindling, minor sound,
That rippled into froth.   Again the quiet
  roll
Of steady notes that surged into a crest
Hung, dropped, and melted with the rest
Into an end that sang within the soul.
I laughed aloud, for eagle-winged and
  bright
I'd sent you flashing through my mighty
  song.
I played it to my friends.   They waited
  long,
Then called it "pretty" ....ah! the
  night
That chilled me, struck my senses numb,
And made my song of you,forever—dumb.

Katharine Schermerhorn Oliver, 1915.

THE DRAGON LAMP

That night we talked across a table's
    space,
And with a tale of knight and nun I
    sought
To please you. "These pale broideries,"
    I thought,
"This quaint, sweet, measured story will
    efface
Her restlessness." Meanwhile with list-
    less grace
Of curving wrist and cool white hand, you
    wrought
Havoc amid the lamp's red fringe; you
    caught
The sinuous dragon pattern on the base,
With drooping glance retraced it. Once,
    forgetting
My silver tale a breathless instant, letting
Your widening eyes sink through the
    morphean maze

To where in dim, deep bronze your own
  tense gaze
Answered, you shrank back from the glow
  afraid.
"The nun can't have been young," you
  softly said.

Louise Hunting Seaman, 1915.

LONDON CHIMNEY POTS

London, London chimney pots,
In the twilight sky,
Rows and rows of chimney pots
To mark the houses by.
Pleasant London chimney pots
Looking down at me,
Can you smell the jasmine
By my apple tree?

Can you hear the children sing
T'other side my hedge,
Singing to the baby moon
Showing one white edge,
"Hokey pokey starlight
Round the moon you go"—
London, London chimney pots,
Is't a song you know?

Vivian Gurney, 1915.

MAN MENDING A PIPE

The lowbrowed tunnel is baking black
With a grimy blackness that smears his
    face,
And dries his nose with its blasting stench,
And pushes his eye-balls out of their
    place;
All in the gulp of a breath.
He drinks it down till this dusty death
Is the native life of his dusty lungs.
The thin blood pounds in his crowded
    head,
Or the hot steam batters against the
    bungs;
It's all the same in the choking dark.
The spot-light cleaves a finger-mark
And wavers against the retreating night.
The steam pipes and their shadows crawl,
Little and big, against the wall,
From the roughcast ceiling spiders fall,
And pale bugs scuttle out of the light.
He crouches onward a weary space,

Searches and finds the broken pipe.
His hot eyes strain on the tiny crack,
The darkness presses against his back,
Eternity hangs between the clack
Of one steam-pipe and the next.

Low and dusty and close and flat,
The tunnel stifles him in its gripe.
He shares its life with his brother the rat—
His work of the world in a broken pipe.

Elizabeth Mason Heath, 1916.

LOVE SONG

There are some things too wonderful to
    tell;
  Sunset, red-gold, across a waveless sea;
  'Twixt pool and pool a glen-stream's
    revelry;
The morning star's pale fire and breath-
    less spell;
And so I cannot say how wonderful you
    are.

There are some things too beautiful to
    know;
  The silver song the shimmering planets
    sing;
  What the tall bending birch is whisper-
    ing;
How sunlight kisses the shy buds a-blow.
So I can only guess your beauty from
    afar!

Carolyn Crosby Wilson, 1917.

CIRCE

He stood before her tall and very strong.
The swine and tigers crouched about her
    feet
And licked them.
His glance upon her was indifferent,
Whereat her gray eyes blazed with sud-
    den joy,
Eager she stretched her arms out, radiant,
Her mouth grown sweet and tender, all
    her form
Trembling with hope. Her very smile
    rejoiced,
Then quivered at his kindled look.
E'er he had reached the spot where yet
    she stood
Her joy had smouldered out.
"Your eyes are like a beast's," young
    Circe said.

Elizabeth Jane Coatsworth, 1915.

THE LOVER

Ah yes
My dearest,
How well I guess
That your slim soul
Reaches out shyly
Toward that same goal
Whence mine has fled.
I panted to the heights and found that
    there
Though brave my aim, my soul
Eternity without you did not dare.
Well, we are here together, just for once.
Your eyes brush past me straining to the
    height,
While I who won and lost because of you,
Powerless watch you pass.
I scorn your purity,
Your eager zeal.
I long to feel
Life surge about me,

Not forget,
As you forget me here.
You are a holy fool.
And yet I love you.

Elizabeth Jane Coatsworth, 1915.
Katharine Schermerhorn Oliver, 1915.

REBELLION

Always when Absalom returned at night,
Tired from hunting, yet adventure-filled,
'Twas Michal met him in the darkened
    court,
Gave him his wine and listened to his
    tales.
Seldom looked she at him from lowered
    lids
But slow spoke words of praise he learned
    to love.
When at bright noon he wandered in the
    groves
Or lay in meditation 'neath a tree
Michal would chance to meet him as she
    walked—
Michal, the queen, daughter of Saul was
    she.
David, the king, never beheld her face
Since she rebuked him; yet she never
    wept
For that she lived a widow while a wife—

She never spoke of those her five young
    sons
Whom David gave to death, nor of her
    house
Whose very name was seldom on men's
    lips
So it had fallen before David's power—
Instead,
She listened to the tales of David's son,
Her white face near his eager beauteous-
    ness—
Or told him he was fair that he was
    strong,
The people loved him more than the
    King's self,
It was a grief to her he was not heir.
And while she spoke with lips that scarce-
    ly moved,
Her eyes kept watch of him 'neath lower-
    ed lids.

Elizabeth Jane Coatsworth, 1915.

CATHLEEN NI HOULIHAN

(In imitation of the poems of Egan O'Rahilly)

When the yellow sun set on the hill
And the mist crept up from the meadow
Did you see the Lady Cathleen,
As you came from the west, from the
    moorland?
It was close by the wind-swept dune,
At sunset I saw her.
Fair is she, fair among maidens.
The red of her hair is the color
Of willows when comes the March wind,
Bringing Spring in her bosom.
Her eyes, ah who can describe them
Save one who has seen in the dark fairy
    well of Killaha
Heaven reflected, a flame in still water?
When she smiled my heart sang with
    delight;
When she weeps—ah then I die for her.

Miriam S. Wright, 1918.

THE DEFIANCE OF LILITH

Swift searched they the universe, track-
    ing down Lilith—
Sennoi, Sansennoi and Sammargeloph,
God-sent and terrible, bright-winged with
    fire
Searched they for Lilith who dared defy
    Godhead,
Utter Shem-hamphorash, Dread Name
    of Names,
And, armed with might by that word un-
    speakable
Scorned great Jehovah, cursed Adam's
    seed—
Adam who hated her, loved her, and
    fawned to her—
Then disappeared from the eyes of the
    Lord.
Fearing her power, remembering her
    beauty,
The strong fierce will of her, turned they
    from Eden

Left Adam smiling, Eve close beside
  him—
Through the three worlds searched they
  for Lilith,
Sennoi, Sansennoi and Sammargeloph.

Elizabeth Jane Coatsworth, 1915.

AUTUMN

Spring, teasing cumbrous Winter from
    her place,
First charms me with her ever changing
    face,
Now with a tear, yet oftener with a smile
She doth beguile
My dancing feet
Into some pleasant, blossom-bowered re-
    treat.

And yet, when lazy, lavish Summer lies
And smiles upon me through her half-
    closed eyes,
Smiles welcome to her wide, reclining
    fields,
Then my heart yields
To her sly wooing,
And drowsy minstrels shrill my sweet
    undoing.

Until, one day, I catch the sudden flare
Of glorious Autumn's wind-blown, flam-
    ing hair.

Her swift step stirs the rustling leaves,
    and then
I meet again
The wishful glow
Of steady, azure eyes; and straightway
    go
Into glad arms, outstretched, yet wearied
    not
With long desire, and only half forgot.

Then Spring and Summer child and wan-
    ton are,
And Autumn my true love returned from
    afar.

Carolyn Crosby Wilson, 1917.

THE DREAMER

I ride on the riotous clouds of dawn
And the roughened waves of the sea.
I know how the horns of the moon are
    made
And the grey crag's mystery.
Borne aloft by the whirlwind's rage
I rush through eternity.

Elsie Lanier, 1918.

Puer quis ex aula capillis
Ad cyathum statuetur unctis,
Doctus sagittas tendere Sericas
Arcu paterno
                    Horace C. I. 29.

Sometimes while passing round the fra-
    grant wine
Fierce memory strikes. Quivering, he
    stands erect,
Longing to tear aside the tunic soft,
Fling on instead the roughened tiger
    skin,
To dash the marble cup upon the ground,
And free, to force a way to Seric plains—

But stifling breath of many-petalled rose
Envelops him. He droops, until he meets
The narrow smile of some dark Latin
    girl,
Onward he glides, off'ring with servile
    grace
Pomegranates, grapes, and sweet Faler-
    nian.   *Agnes Rogers,* 1916.

PROLOGUE

(*From the Pageant of Athena. Written and presented
by the Students of Vassar College at their Fiftieth
Anniversary Exercises, October, 1915.*)

Athena speaks :

Bright in the skein of time gleam many
    strands,
Endlessly varied. I have chosen those
Of flame, of fire, of rich luxuriant gold,
And those whose beauty lies in their clear
    strength.
My will it is to weave them, strand on
    strand,
Tracing the course of learning through
    the years
In one close wrought design. All those
    who come
Shall pause before this fabric, ages old,
Shaped by past lives in symmetry and
    truth,

And glorying in design so well begun,
Themselves shall add thereto.   And this
  my web
Shall weaving be forever, never done.

ALTA MATER

What gifts ask we at thy fair hands?
Thy love what grace imparts?
The will to dare, the hand to do,
Thy light within our hearts.

High, Mother, is thy heart,
As thy gray tower's height.
Strong, Mother, are thy hands,
Thy torch burns ever bright.

What gifts lay we at thy fair feet,
Since we are greatly blest?
Our strength, our hope, to bear thy light
Undimmed from east to west.

High, Mother, is thy heart,
As thy gray tower's height.
Strong, Mother, are thy hands,
Thy torch burns ever bright.

Elizabeth Mason Heath, 1916.

DAWN

At the feet of his lady the moon
  Lies the night.
Aquiver and breathless and bright,
    With the light
  Of her smile on his face,
And the shadows her slim fingers trace.

And now she is gone, and he lies
Black browed and brooding and still;
    And over the hill
      From afar
    The clear morning star
Burns but to set him a-thrill.
    But the night steals away
Seeking his lady, and leaves the star, pal-
    ing, with day.

Carolyn Crosby Wilson, 1917.

THE SANDMAN

He catches dust o' dreams to carry in his
   sack,
The dust a falling star leaves shining
   in its track,
He walks the milky-way, then down the
   dark-staired skies,
His tinkling footsteps hush the world
   with lullabies.
And when he reaches you, his fragrant
   gentle hands
Fill deep your drowsy eyes with fairy
   golden sands.

Helen Johnson, 1918.

THE FAIRY RING

The fairies' ring is up in the night sky
Around the moon;
And little moonbeams silently dance by
In silver shoon.
The star lamps glow,
The wind sings low
A lullaby,
A fairy tune.
But all the woodland people sigh
For their lost happy ring, and long to fly
To the white moon.

Elizabeth Keller, 1916

ALONE

Under the misty sky, low-hanging, gray,
The hills stretched, dark and still in the
    half light;
The wet air, scented like an April night
With marshy sweetness, on our parched
    lips lay—
Unbroken silence save for the light stir
Of dry, dead grass,
And once, along the forest edge, the whir
Of a gray partridge startled into flight—
I felt the quiet pass
Like balm into my heart. For grief that
    burned
But yesterday, in the mad land of human
    ills,
Here was no place.
Instinctively I turned
To you—and found you staring at the
    hills
And saw the fierce world-hunger in your
    face.

Charlotte Van de Water, 1917.

ROAD SONG

"Seek, seek, but not to find!
Know the lonely heart of the wind,
The rim of the hills with the stars behind,
    And the roads of all the world."

The wind has a home behind the moon,
The little stars sleep in the glare of noon.
I walk alone and my heart is blind,
    On the roads of all the world.

Elizabeth Mason Heath, 1916.

CONFIDANTE

I, who walk in the dark,
Alone beyond all knowing,
Must watch to-night
Glad, sheltered light
In strangers' windows glowing.

Unto me, hungering
With unfulfilled desires,
The keen wind brings
Warm scent of things
That brew by strangers' fires.

I find my darkened house,
Silent and all alone,
And my sup of bread,
That is dry and dead,
And no candle but my own.

Carolyn Crosby Wilson, 1917.

THE SUICIDE

"Curse thee, Life, I will live with thee no
    more!
Thou hast mocked me, starved me, beat
    my body sore!
And all for a pledge that was not pledged
    by me
I have kissed thy crust and eaten sparing-
    ly
That I might eat again, and met thy
    sneers
With deprecations, and thy blows with
    tears,—
Aye, from thy glutted lash, glad, crawl-
    ed away,
As if spent passion were a holiday!
And now I go. Nor threat, nor easy
    vow
Of tardy kindness can avail thee now
With me, whence fear and faith alike
    are flown;
Lonely I came, and I depart alone,

And know not where nor unto whom I
go;
But that thou canst not follow me I
know."

Thus I to Life, and ceased; but through
my brain
My thought ran still, until I spake again:

"Ah, but I go not as I came,—no trace
Is mine to bear away of that old grace
I brought! I have been heated in thy
fires,
Bent by thy hands, fashioned to thy
desires,
Thy mark is on me! I am not the same
Nor ever more shall be, as when I came.

Ashes am I of all that once I seemed.
In me all's sunk that leapt, and all that
dreamed
Is wakeful for alarm,—oh, shame to thee,
For the ill change that thou hast wrought
in me,
Who laugh no more nor lift my throat
to sing!

Ah, Life, I would have been a happy
thing
To have about the house when I was
grown
If thou hadst left my little joys alone!
I asked of thee no favor, save this one;
That thou wouldst leave me playing in
the sun!
And this thou didst deny, calling my
name
Insistently, until I rose and came.
I saw the sun no more. * * * *It were
not well
So long on these unpleasant thoughts
to dwell,
Need I arise tomorrow and renew
Again my hated tasks, but I am through
With all things save my thoughts and
this one night,
So that in truth I seem already quite
Free and remote from thee,—I feel no
haste
And no reluctance to depart; I taste,
Merely, with thoughtful mien, an un-
known draught,

That in a little while I shall have quaff-
ed."
Thus I to Life, and ceased, and slightly
smiled,
Looking at nothing! and my thin dreams
filed
Before me one by one till once again
I set new words unto an old refrain:

"Treasures thou hast that never have
been mine!
Warm lights in many a secret chamber
shine
Of thy gaunt house, and gusts of song
have blown
Like blossoms out to me that sat alone!
And I have waited well for thee to show
If any share were mine,—and now I go!
Nothing I leave, and if I naught attain
I shall but come into mine own again!"

Thus I to Life, and ceased, and spake
no more,
But, turning, straightway sought a cer-
tain door
In the rear wall. Heavy it was, and low

And dark,—a way by which none e'er
  would go
That other exit had, and never knock
Was heard thereat,—bearing a curious
  lock
Some chance had shown me fashioned
  fcultily,
Whereof Life held, content, the useless
  key,
And great coarse hinges, thick and rough
  with rust,
Whose sudden voice across a silence
  must,
I knew, be harsh and horrible to hear,—
A strange door, ugly like a dwarf.
  So near
I came I felt upon my feet the chill
Of a dread wind creeping across the sill.
So stood longtime, till over me at last
Came weariness, and all things other
  passed
To make it room; the still night drifted
  deep
Like snow about me, and I longed for
  sleep.

But suddenly, marking the morning
  hour,
Bayed the deep-throated bell within
  the tower!
Startled, I raised my head,—and with
  a shout
Laid hold upon the latch,—and was
  without.

* * * * * * * *

Ah, long-forgotten, well-remembered
  road,
Leading me back unto my old abode,
My father's house! There in the night
  I came,
And found them feasting, and all things
  the same
As they had been before. A splendor
  hung
Upon the walls, and such sweet songs
  were sung
As, echoing out of very long ago,
Had called me from the house of Life,
  I know.
So fair their raiment shone I looked in
  shame

On the unlovely garb in which I came!
Then straightway at my hesitancy mock-
ed:
"It is my father's house!" I said, and
knocked;
And the door opened. To the shining
crowd,
Tattered and dark I entered, like a cloud,
Seeing no face but his; to him I crept,
And "Father!" I cried, and clasped his
knees, and wept.

Ah, days of joy that followed! All alone
I wandered through the house. My
own, my own,
My own to touch, my own to taste and
smell,
All I had lacked so long and loved so
well!
None shook me out of sleep, none hush-
ed my song,
None called me in from the sunlight all
day long.

I know not when the wonder came to me
Of what my father's business might be,

And whither fared and on what errands
  bent
The tall and gracious messengers he
  sent.
Yet one day with no song from dawn till
  night
Wondering I sat and watched them out
  of sight.
And the next day I called; and on the
  third
Asked them if I might go,—but no one
  heard.

Then, sick with longing, I arose at last
And went unto my father,—in that vast
Chamber wherein he for so many years
Has sat, surrounded by his charts and
  spheres.
"Father," I said, "Father, I cannot play
The harp that thou didst give me; and
  all day
I sit in idleness, while to and fro
About me thy serene, grave servants go;
And I am weary of my lonely ease.
Better a perilous journey overseas

133

Away from thee, than this, the life I
   lead,
To sit all day in the sunshine like a weed
That grows to naught,—I love thee
   more than they
Who serve thee most; yet serve thee in
   no way.
Father, I beg of thee a little task
To dignify my days,—'tis all I ask
Forever, but forever, this denied,
I perish."
   "Child," my father's voice replied,
"All things thy fancy hath desired of me
Thou hast received. I have prepared
   for thee
Within my house a spacious chamber,
   where
Are delicate things to handle and to
   wear,
And all these things are thine. Dost
   thou love song?
My minstrels shall attend thee all day
   long.
Or sigh for flowers? My fairest gar-
   dens stand

Open as fields to thee on every hand.
And all thy days this word shall hold
the same:
No pleasure shalt thou lack that thou
shalt name.
But as for tasks"—he smiled, and shook
his head:
"Thou hadst thy task, and laidst it by,"
he said.

Edna St. Vincent Millay, 1917.

AN ETCHING

A grey ship sails into a misty sky.
Grey sea gulls tipped with white go circl-
    ing by.
Oh, ship! so like my life you seem to me,
Grey life against a grey eternity.
Oh, sea gulls! like the years you circling
    fly,
Grey years white tipped with dreams
    that soar so high.
Oh, ship, that you might rest against the
    sky
While sea gulls tipped with white go circl-
    ing by!

Elsie Lanier, 1918.

ATTAINMENT

To reach the top you strove;
You only saw brown earth that backward
swept
Beneath your feet;
Above—beyond—the slim path dodged
and leapt,
Than you a thousand times more fleet,
To lose itself in yon high-clinging grove.

High up, a mountain spring
Tossed its clear crystal freely down to you,
With silken shiver,
Shattered on every jagged rock anew,
You only said, "Ah, here's a river;
I'll quench my thirst; 'twill aid my labor-
ing."

A free wind from the crown
Of other distant hills swept by and stir-
red
The waiting trees;

With pleasant quivers of surprise they
  heard
That you were near; you said, "The
  breeze
Is good for climbing. Hope it won't die
  down."

Why, when the day was cool
On some poised cliff could you not pause,
  and there
With grateful eye
Scan the walled reaches of the valley fair;
Or see unfathomable sky
Gaze back from an unfathomed mountain
  pool?

Thought you through pressing clouds the
  open sky to gain?
Drenched is the summit with close mists
  and sleet-sharp rain!

Carolyn Crosby Wilson, 1917.

WIND RHYTHM

The moonlight glimmers in a pale green
film on the frozen creek and the snow-
covered hill beyond. Along the creek
stand slender trees, their bare branches
dark against the thinly-clouded, violet
sky. Fine black twigs quiver across the
mist-blurred moon. The wind rises in
the heavy firs that droop their branches
on the hill;

"Sound and swell,
    Sound and swell,
Rocking slow, rocking slow."
It reaches the slender trees;
"Swirl and sway,
    Swirl and sway,
Bending low, bending low."
Now the little twigs are caught by the
    wind;
"Falter and fling,
    Falter and fling,
Wildly blow, wildly blow."

Elizabeth Mary Hincks, 1917.

139

UNSEEN

In the blind darkness of unlit rooms
I was groping,
My curious finger-tips seeking elusive
    things.
When a touch like the breath of a violet
Brushed me—and was gone.

The myst'ry of delicate moth-wings held
    me
In thrall.
Hope whispered to me of the open path
    to the dream-world,
Of wee sylphs in petal-soft dress.
I waited—
Then tenderly sought
In the silence, scarce breathing my prayer
For that dream-caress.

Once more it trembled near me—

The spell of all enchanted things was just
    beyond my finger-tips.
Softly I crushed it to hold forever
—A narcissus, frail-petalled and dead.

Bee W. Hasler, 1917.

MID-WINTER

If I were God, I'd mould hills rolling low,
Smooth them and shape them, sift them
    deep with snow,
And scatter them with furze that they
    might lie
Softly against the wide, deep-tinted sky.
In slow caress my forming hand would
    linger,
Then a swift finger,
Down some long slope, half carelessly
    would break
A jagged course for melting snows to
    take.
The out-scooped valley's length they'd
    run and then'
Skirting new hills, go slipping out of ken.
And distanced far, a low–hung sun I'd
    light,
And paint blue shadows on the rose-
    touched white

142

Then, wearied, put aside my colors and
   my clay,
And fashion paradise and man on some
   less perfect day.

Carolyn Crosby Wilson, 1917.

AT RANDOM
(A Department of Nonsense)

DRESS A LA CARTE

'Tis Friday night, but customs change,
How college doth progress!
And so though pie is on the plate
I wear my ice cream dress!

NOTHING AT ALL

She was a tall and goodly Senior,
  I was an innocent Freshman small,
I met her one night in the Ethics alcove,
  That was all.

She was a spectacled Greek professor,
  I was an innocent freshman small,
I asked in the hall, "Do you do our sweep-
    ing?"
  That was all.

He was a gas-man, pleasantly smiling,
  I was an innocent freshman small,
I only asked him to change my schedule,
  That was all.

It was a beautiful senior parlor,
  I was an innocent freshman small,
It looked so nice I stepped inside it,
  That was all.

Then why do they laugh and point the
    finger
At me, an innocent freshman small?
I'm only asking for information,
    That is all.

F. L. McK., 1898.

LAMENT

The Vassar student well displays
  Her slothful disposition
She twines about the classroom chairs
  In serpentine position.

In Sunday Evening Music, too,
  She finds it much more pleasing
To lie recumbent on the seat,
  Her weary soul thus easing.

In such wild ways she will persist,
  It tears my soul asunder;
Do you suppose she thinks it's *nice*?
  I wonder, oh, I wonder —

K. T., 1910.

IRONY

I thought that it was fit
For me to study up a bit
  On the Ec. conditions of the working
    class;
But just lately I have learned
That my study must be turned
  To an Ec. condition of my own, alas!

THE LEADING MAN

"Oh isn't the leading man good?
Her voice—" "And his gestures, my dear.
He is more like herself when he smiles,
But doesn't her moustache look queer?"
"He is only pretending to smoke;
Those puffs—" "Come from her powder-
can.
And when she makes love to the girl,"
"She is the most wonderful man!"

I. U., 1910.

MY SOUL

My soul is like an alley cat
Long, mangy, lank and thin;
It never feeds on porterhouse
But from the garbage tin.

O Thou, who feedest hungry souls
And seek'st to make them fat,
I pray that Thou mayst make my soul
A house—not alley-cat.

Then may it, sleeping, purr alway,
Calm in its sleek rotundity,
A boul'vard soul, and boul'vard fed,
A perfect soul, the soul of me!

R. P. L., 1913.

SONNET TO A HAIRPIN

Implement of beauty and of use!
Female Adorner! At such waste I frown-
ed
When first I saw thee broken on the
ground,
Dropped by some "libe" ward maid;
with tresses loose
Onward she fled and murmured low, "The
Deuce".
In thousands since, the pretty shell I've
found,
In millions, meeker ones in wire gowned,
Oh stay of locks! How great is thy abuse!

Yet some who shed thee most have learned
in "Ec."
(Or other class) that use is one great
force
And beauty t'other, to keep life's craft
afloat.

These lost and gone, the ship is like to
    leak.
But careless, thee they drop along their
    course,
Knowing thy gifts.   And yet they wish
    the vote!

M. M., 1915.

A PSYCHOLOGICAL DISILLUSION

They said it was a "cinchy", three lectures
    a week
And nothing she'd tell you was new—
The quizzes were easy, and in the half-
    year
  There were only three topics to do.

So I signed for the stuff with a smile on
    my face,
In college such joy rides are few.
And the first weeks slipped by, while I
    worked not at all
  I had only three topics to do.

Then came round a week-end I meant to
    begin,
But I found I'd a theme overdue,
A tea and a lecture; my worry was small
  With only three topics to do.

A trip to New York, a Hall Play, a guest,
My conscience began to pursue

And poison my mind with the ghost of the
   thought
There were still those three topics to do.

Though I've worked like a Trojan to find
   some spare time,
In a week the semester is through—
And with all my reviewing and several
   long themes
I've still those three topics to do.

H. E. B., 1917.

THE BALLAD OF BAD 'BACCY

Where Market and the Main Street meet
  In U. C. S. shop quite replete
With every sort of smoky treat,
  I'm working.
One day there came a maiden sweet
On neat and hesitating feet,
And her remarks I now repeat
  Sans shirking.

"I want" said she, "kind sir, to get
A mild but mellow cigarette
That's pleasant for to smell, and yet
  Has pep."
Whereat I did proceed to slip
Her scented things with golden tip
And winked, as who would say, quite flip,
  "I'm hep."

Her look would make your heart to bleed,
"I do not smoke the filthy weed,"
Said she, "I will explain my need
  Of nicotine.

For in my dormitory cellar
There lives and smokes a wretched fellar,
A silent subterranean dweller,
   Who's never seen.

"And through my register a fume
Each morning floods my sitting-room,
And wraps me close in smoke and gloom
   All day.
And if from morn till eve I choke,
And folks all think 'tis I who smoke
I'm going to choose the brand—or croak,
   I say!"

Said I, "Fatimas or Pell Mell
Are famous for their pleasant smell
But I've a plan that works as well—
   Retire him!
Go to the folks the help that hire,
And with this motto raise their ire,
'There is no smoke without a fire—
   So fire him!'"

C. C. W., 1917.

PISCIS VASSARIAE

Ent'ring the dining room in doubt,
And gazing hopefully about,
On every hand I hear a shout,
"I pass!" 'By me!" and "One without!"

Seeking my place I quickly feel
A touch upon my arm.   I wheel.
A stranger queries at my heel
"Do they play bridge at every meal?"

A gentle guest—I would not sass her—
For I was once as simple as her,
And so, I murmur as I pass her—
"It is the day for fish at Vassar."

C. C. W., 1917.

FLUNCTURE

Once 'twas an oyster gaunt and pallid
Enmeshed in coils of macaroni;
And once it was a salmon sallid;
And once 'twas fish both strong and boni.

And once the heat came on at noon;
And once it never came at all;
And once it waned, as wanes the moon,
When Fahrenheit began, to fall.

And once I flunked me flat in Ethics;
And once I flunked in Mathematics.

———

Who was it flunked in Dietetics?
Who was it flunked in Thermostatics?

C. C. W., 1917.

THE OLD ORDER CHANGETH

The first bell rang at dawn of day;
The air was chill, the sky was grey;
  I would have slept.
The bed was cozy where I lay,
And my first class three hours away;
  Yet up I leapt.

Into my roomy's room I sped
And slammed the window by her bed;
  In accents gay
"Get up, it's pancake day," I said.
She pulled the covers round her head—
  "We had them yesterday!"

                    C. C. W., 1917.

WHY DID I EVER COME TO
THIS PLACE?

(An expedition in untrammelled verse)

Sometimes
When the eight o'clock bell rings,
And the maids,
In a long, black, frantic line,
Scurry from the dining-room
Like rats
From a doomed ship,
(Nor will any of them catch my eye
Though I have been waiting
As patient as a farmer's wife
Since dawn)
I say to myself,
Or to any who cares to listen,
That college is a bore,
And that woman's place
Is in the home.

And again,
When the chapel chimes,

Forgetting that it is TOWN SUNDAY,
(Or uninformed)
Ding,
That is to say, "peal",
For quite some time,
As blithe,
And inexorable,
And out of tune,
As anybody else in a bath-tub,
(Or as foolishly complacent
As a football player
Who runs in the wrong direction
And scores a goal
For the other side)
I turn in bed,
And glare at the plaster, which is scarred
By generations of thumb-tacks,
For whose insertion I,
As guiltless
As is a Freshman of knowledge,
Do semi-annually
Settle,
And I say to myself,
Or to the servant who comes in just then
To empty the waste-basket,

That college
Is the misapprehension
Of a June-bug mind,
And that woman's place
Is in the home.

And always
When with some youth,
Whom I do not love,
But might,
In the proper environment,
I have trudged for hours,
Pointing out the Library
And the Art Building,
Over and over,
(For the parlors
Are full of parents,
And five room-mates
Are an insufficient chaperone)
Always
I say to myself,
Or to the night-watchman,
Who does not care,
That I wish I were happily married
To a dyspeptic widower

With six small children,
And that higher education for women
Is as paradoxical a quantity
As prohibition at election time,
And that woman's place
Is in the home.

E. St. V. M., 1917.

PARTIALITY

I don't care much for water snakes and
  wiry centipedes,
It seems to be a footless life the solemn
  fishworm leads,
In fact, the crawling creatures that appeal
  to me are few—
But I love the gentle Caterpillar, snuggl-
  ing in my shoe.

The reason for this preference is very
  plainly shown,
'Tis not for outside beauty, and his soul
  is little known,
Still I love the Caterpillar—'tis love re-
  turned, you see,
Because the gentle creature is so very
  fond of *me*.

For he scrambles up the instep of *my* foot,
  or in *my* hair,
And if he wants to take a snooze, t's
  always in *my* chair,

So I love the gentle Caterpillar dearly as
can be—
Were there but one in all the land, he'd
surely crawl on *me*.

M. A. P., 1905.

HUMANITY

Tread lightly on the humble bug,
    Step gently on the worm,
And dry their tears and calm their fears
    And soothe them when they squirm.

L. B., 1907.

HUMILITY

But should a big bug cross your path,
    Give place, with lowered eye.
Let not a word from you be heard
    Till it has passed you by.

E. B. D., 1909.

BUG OF JUNE

O bug of June that comest still
When blossomed verdure clothes the hill,
To thee my warblings I indite,
Proud monarch of the sultry night.

The campus glowing in the noon
Is not thy province, bug of June.
Thou wait'st till in the dying day
Allures thee forth the droplight's ray.

Thou buzzest in my private cup,
My honey gives thee royal sup,
Three room-mates lying in a swoon,
Proclaim thy power, bug of June!

Strong enough my filial loyalty
To Alma Mater, yet for me
The end cannot arrive too soon—
With freedom from thee, bug of June!

V. L. B., 1911.

A VALENTINE

If I were but a lovely worm
Which had a graceful, wiggly tail,
My prepossessing, pretty squirm,
To win your heart would never fail.
I'd tie myself in knots for you,
Or coyly wrinkle up my skin,
Or stretch myself a foot or two
As straight and slender as a pin.
I'd let you bait your hook with me
And gladly toss myself about
'Til all the fishes in the sea
Thought me the worm of worms, no doubt.
But, if you held me in your hand,
Still as the great stone sphinx I'd lie,
Nor any greater joy demand
Before I curled me up to die.

M. H., 1912.

THE CENTIPEDE

Of all the terrors of the night that make
    one's flesh to crawl
The worst it is the centipede that walketh
    on the wall.
Of all the dangers of the day that chill one
    to the core
The worst it is the centipede that fleeth
    o'er floor.
Of all the horrors of dawn and dusk that
    wring one on the rack
The worst it is the centipede that crawleth
    from the crack.

One finds him in one's teacup, in one's
    bathtub, and one's bed,
And he drops quick from the ceiling on
    one's unsuspecting head,
And his wiggly legs still wiggle after one
    has squashed him dead.
He leaves a gooey brownish stain upon
    one's smooth cream wall
When his crawly self is blotted out and
    nevermore will crawl;

Ah, yes, alive or dead he is of known beasts
    worst of all!
Sometimes when I am working in my
    chamber late at night
And look up at my wall with murders
    spotted, by dim light
Each deathplace seems to move and crawl
    —it is a ghastly sight.
And far up near the ceiling where the gay
    mosquito hies
Faint moving dots reveal themselves as
    spiders, moths, and flies,
How deep I love their so few legs for this
    so sweet surprise.

Perhaps the cause of centipedes in the
    great scheme of nature
Is just to teach us heartfelt joy for every
    other creature.
For of all the beasts in all the world that
    craze one's soul with fear
The worst is sure the centipede that is
    my roommate here.

E. K., 1916

SPRING SONG

Worms! How I hate them writhing in the
  rain
On all the paths from Josselyn to Main!
And how I hate the slimy way they feel,
Cringing and crushed beneath a rubber
  heel!
And how I hate the bloated way they
  squirm—
See! There are twins and there is half a
  worm!

C. C. W., 1917.

Printed in the United States
101532LV00007B/62/A